The Liberty Bell

Debra Hess

BENCHMARK BOOKS

MARSHALL CAVENDISH
NEW YORK

Benchmark Books
Marshall Cavendish
99 White Plains Road
Tarrytown, NY 10591-9001
www.marshallcavendish.com

Library of Congress Cataloging-in-Publication Data
Hess, Debra.
 The Liberty Bell / by Debra Hess.
    p. cm. — (Symbols of America)
Summary: Traces the history of the Liberty Bell, including its role in the American Revolution, its famous crack, and how it became a symbol of the United States.
Includes bibliographical references and index.
 ISBN 0-7614-1713-3
 1. Liberty Bell—Juvenile literature. 2. Philadelphia (Pa.)—Buildings, structures, etc.—Juvenile literature.
 [1. Liberty Bell. 2. Philadelphia (Pa.)—Buildings, structures, etc.] I. Title. II. Series: Hess, Debra. Symbols of America.

F158.8.I3H47 2003
974.8'11—dc21

2003004463

Photo research by Anne Burns Images

Cover photo: Corbis/Lester Lefkowitz
Back cover: Photri

All the photographs in this book are used with permission and through the courtesy of:
Corbis: Leif Skoogfors, title page; Dennis Degnan, 7; Bob Krist, 11, 28; Bettman, 35. *Photri:* Jeff Greenburg, 4; 15, 23, 31. *Granger Collection:* 8, 12, 24. *North Wind Pictures:* 16, 19, 20, 27, 32.

Series design by Adam Mietlowski

Printed in Italy

1 3 5 6 4 2

Contents

CHAPTER ONE

A Cracked Bell

There is a bell in Philadelphia, Pennsylvania, that is known around the world. It is a famous American symbol. It is also famous for the zigzag crack that runs down its side. Because of this crack, the Liberty Bell has not *tolled* for more than 150 years.

In the 1700s there were no computers, televisions, radios, or telephones. It was difficult to spread important news from one town to another. Bells were one way people *communicated* with each other. Bells were rung to call people together. Citizens would gather in the center of town when they heard the bells ring, and the news would be read out loud. Bells also warned people of danger such as fire or enemy attack.

◄ *Every year visitors flock to Philadelphia to see—and touch—the Liberty Bell.*

In 1751 the people of the Pennsylvania colony decided they wanted a special bell for their assembly building in Philadelphia. The people called this building the State House even though Pennsylvania was not yet a state. The State House was the place where the assembly, or the people who ran the colony, met to discuss and pass laws important to them. The State House later became known as Independence Hall. The assembly wanted the hall to have a large bell. But there were no bell makers nearby. So the bell had to be ordered from England. It arrived at the end of August 1752 and was hung on March 10, 1753, in a special steeple that had been built to house it.

Independence Hall in Philadelphia is now a national historical park.

A crowd of people gathered in the State House yard, eager to hear the new bell ring. The clapper swung. But instead of the beautiful *pealing* sound everyone expected to hear, there was a terrible clank. The bell had a crack in it.

Did You Know?

• The actual original weight of the Liberty Bell was 2,080 pounds (943 kilograms).
• The *clapper* of the bell weighs 44.5 pounds (20.2 kilograms).

The State House was an important meeting place in colonial Philadelphia. People came from across the city on the day the new bell was rung.

The Pennsylvania assembly decided to send the cracked bell back to England for repairs. But the captain of the British ship said there was no room on board for the bell. Since it could be months before another ship sailed for London, the assembly decided to have the bell fixed in Philadelphia. Two men, John Pass and John Stow, were hired to *cast* a new bell. Very little is known about these two men except that they were local craftsmen. *Historians* have never been able to find out whether either man had any experience in bell casting.

In the 1700s making a bell was hard work. Cracking was a common problem. ▶

John Pass and John Stow broke the bell into small pieces and melted it. Then they added copper to the melted bell to make it stronger. Finally they poured the liquid into a mold and let it harden. In late March 1753 a huge party was held so the people of Philadelphia could hear the ringing of the new bell. But when the bell was rung, people started to laugh and to make jokes. The bell sounded awful. Its ring was not very musical. There was too much copper in the bell. So Pass and Stow decided to try again. They took down the bell and melted it. This time they added tin to the mixture. In early June the new bell was hung and rung once more.

◀ *In honor of their effort, the Liberty Bell bears the names of its makers, John Pass and John Stow.*

While Pass and Stow's second bell was more musical than the first, it was still not what the assembly had hoped for. So a new bell was ordered from England. When that bell arrived, it did not sound much better than the ones Pass and Stow had made. The assembly decided to hang the new British bell in the clock tower anyway. There it chimed to mark the hours of the day.

The bell the Pennsylvania assembly ordered from England was placed in the clock tower of the State House.

▶

Pass and Stow's recast bell stayed in the steeple. It became the official Pennsylvania State House bell. It was rung to call people to the State House to hear news. It was also rung to announce assembly meetings and sessions of the courts. It was rung all the time. People began to complain. They thought the bell rang too often and was too loud. They said the constant ringing was harmful to sick people and could prevent them from getting well again. They wanted the ringing to stop. But the assembly ignored the request and kept ringing the bell anyway.

After a while, the ringing of the new bell in the State House started to annoy people who lived nearby.

CHAPTER TWO

The American Revolution

In 1775 the thirteen American colonies went to war with England to win their *independence*. The next year, each of the colonies sent *delegates* to a meeting in Philadelphia. There they wrote the Declaration of Independence, and the United States of America was born. The Declaration of Independence was read to the public for the first time on July 8, 1776, in the yard of the Pennsylvania State House. When the reading was over, the bell rang, and the crowd cheered.

A large crowd gathered in front of the Pennsylvania State House to hear the first reading of the Declaration of Independence.

▶

The war for independence would not be easy. England did not want to let its American colonies go. In the fall of 1777, all signs pointed to a British invasion of Philadelphia. The new American *Congress* was sure that if the bell fell into enemy hands, it would be melted to make cannons and *ammunition*. So they hid it along with ten other city bells. When the British marched into Philadelphia on September 26, 1777, they found that all the bells were missing.

Here, a colonist tears down the king's arms from above the door of the State House. The people of Philadelphia wanted to remove this symbol of England's control over the American colonies.

American colonel Benjamin Flower had been given the important job of hiding the bells. He put them in farm wagons and covered them with straw and sacks. The State House Bell rode in a wagon belonging to a farmer named John Jacob Mickley. The farm wagons blended in with the 700 British army wagons that were also leaving town. Eventually, the bell was hidden beneath the floor of the Zion Reformed Church in Allentown, Pennsylvania.

For several years, most of Philadelphia's bell towers and steeples stood empty. Colonists hid the Liberty Bell in nearby Allentown. ▶

The bell stayed hidden until the British decided to move their army north to New York on June 18, 1778. After the British left, the bell was returned to the State House steeple. But by 1781 the wood had rotted, and the steeple needed to be torn down. Workers lowered the bell to the part of the bell tower that was made of sturdy brick. The bell was rung for the first time from its new location on October 24, 1781, to mark the surrender of the British army at Yorktown, Virginia. The Americans had won the Revolutionary War.

The British surrendered to American forces on October 19, 1781, at Yorktown, Virginia. The war was finally over.

The bell stayed in the tower for almost the next seventy years. It was rung in 1783 when a peace *treaty* was signed with England. Four years later it tolled when the *Constitution* of the United States was *ratified*. On the Fourth of July that year, the bell also rang out in celebration of America's newfound liberty. In 1799 Pennsylvania made Lancaster its state capital. The State House Bell, however, stayed in Philadelphia. It was used to call voters, to mourn important deaths, and to celebrate the Fourth of July each year. But it no longer rang every day.

Did You Know?

Many people think Pennsylvania is spelled wrong on the Liberty Bell. The state's name appears as "Pensylvania." But unlike today, in the 1700s, Pennsylvania was often spelled with only one *n*.

Independence Hall is often called a birthplace of American freedom. The U.S. Constitution was signed there in 1787. George Washington led the group that wrote the important document.

No one is sure when the Liberty Bell cracked. Many think it was on July 8, 1835, when it was rung to mourn the death of John Marshall, chief justice of the Supreme Court. After that day, the Liberty Bell hung broken and silent for many years. Then, in 1846, two churches began competing for the honor of ringing their bells to celebrate George Washington's birthday. Instead, it was decided that the Liberty Bell would ring to mark the special day. Workers drilled the bell's crack to keep the edges from *vibrating* against each other. It was thought that this would prevent the crack from getting bigger. But on February 22, 1846, the bell was rung for Washington's birthday and cracked beyond repair. It was the last time the Liberty Bell would ever ring.

To preserve the Liberty Bell for future visitors, officials decided in 1846 that this important American symbol must never be rung again.

CHAPTER THREE

A Symbol of Freedom

There are words from the Bible *engraved* in a circle at the top of the Liberty Bell. They read: "Proclaim liberty throughout all the land unto all the inhabitants [residents] thereof." This means that the bell's purpose is to announce freedom to everyone who lives in America. In late 1837 a drawing of the bell appeared on the cover of a publication named *Liberty*. This small magazine supported the *abolition* of slavery. Two years later another anti-slavery magazine, called the *Liberator*, printed a copy of a poem about the bell. The poem was called "The Liberty Bell." Ever since, the bell has been known by that name.

The words engraved on the Liberty Bell serve as a message of freedom. ▶

Although it has not rung in more than 150 years, the Liberty Bell remains a symbol of freedom throughout the world. It has traveled across America. In 1893 it was shown at the Chicago world's fair. In 1915 it traveled to San Francisco after thousands of schoolchildren signed a *petition* asking that the bell be sent as part of the city's *exposition*. This was the last time the Liberty Bell left Philadelphia.

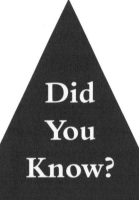

Did You Know?

The Liberty Bell is well traveled! Each time it was displayed at a fair or exposition, crowds of people came out to greet it. People organized parades and hired bands to play—even if the bell stopped only for a few minutes before moving on. The bell was sent by train. Between 1885 and 1915, the Liberty Bell traveled to 8 world's fairs and stopped at almost 400 cities along the way.

◀ *The Liberty Bell was a popular sight at the world's fair in Chicago in 1893.*

For many years, on special occasions such as George Washington's two hundredth birthday in 1932 and the end of World War II in 1945, the Liberty Bell was tapped with a rubber hammer called a mallet. But even a light tapping is not allowed anymore because of the damage it could do to the bell. Until the fall of 2003, the bell stayed silent in a pavilion across the street from Independence Hall. Today the Liberty Bell is housed in the new Liberty Bell Center. More than 1.5 million people visit it each year. They travel from around the world to see a bell that is a symbol of freedom everywhere.

Even a gentle tapping to mark the end of World War II proved too risky for the fragile Liberty Bell. ▶

Glossary

abolition—Putting an end to.

ammunition—Bullets, shells, grenades, bombs, and other things that can be exploded or fired from guns.

cast—To form something by pouring soft material into a mold until it hardens. To recast is to do it again.

clapper—The part of a bell that hangs in the center and strikes the sides when the bell is rung.

communicate—To exchange or express feelings, thoughts, or information.

Congress—The branch of the U.S. government that helps make laws.

Constitution—The document containing the law and plan of the U.S. government.

delegate—Someone who represents a group of people at a meeting.

engrave—To cut a design into metal, wood, or glass.

exposition—A large public show.

historian—A person who studies the past.

independence—Freedom.

peal—To ring.

petition—A document requesting a certain action be taken.

ratify—To adopt officially.

toll—To ring.

treaty—An agreement ending a war.

vibrate—To move rapidly back and forth or up and down.

Find Out More

Books

Binns, Tristan Boyer. *The Liberty Bell*. Crystal Lake, IL: Heinemann, 2001.

Marcovitz, Hal, and Barry Moreno. *The Liberty Bell*. Broomhall, PA: Mason Crest, 2002.

Sakurai, Gail. *The Liberty Bell*. Danbury, CT: Children's Press, 1996.

Slate, Joseph, and Craig Spearing. *The Great Big Wagon That Rang: How the Liberty Bell Was Saved*. Tarrytown, NY: Marshall Cavendish, 2002.

Wilson, Jon. *The Liberty Bell: The Sounds of Freedom*. Chanhassen, MN: Child's World, 1998.

Web Sites

The Liberty Bell
http://www.salem.k12va.us/south/america/bell.htm

The Liberty Bell
http://www.ushistory.org/libertybell

Liberty Bell Craft
http://familycrafts.about.com/library/projects/blbellcr1.htm

Liberty Bell Virtual Museum
http://www.libertybellmuseum.com

Liberty's Kids
http://pbskids.org/libertyskids/arch_where_indepen.html

Index